LETTERS TO
Pope Benedict

COLLEGE STUDENTS SPEAK OUT

EDITED BY

R. John Kinkel, Ph.D.

Oakland University, Rochester, Michigan

Order this book online at www.trafford.com
or email orders@trafford.com

Most Trafford titles are also available at major online book retailers.

Printed in the United States of America.

ISBN: 978-1-4269-7431-1 (sc)
ISBN: 978-1-4269-7432-8 (hc)
ISBN: 978-1-4669-0032-5 (e)

Library of Congress Control Number: 2011917756

Trafford rev. 10/28/2011

 www.trafford.com

North America & international
toll-free: 1 888 232 4444 (USA & Canada)
phone: 250 383 6864 ♦ fax: 812 355 4082

CONTENTS

DEDICATION

Charles W. Bailey (1946-2008)

ACKNOWLEDGMENTS

All books depend on the generosity and cooperation of numerous individuals. I am grateful to the many students who took pen in hand and boldly spoke out about their ideas concerning the Catholic Church. I know it took time and effort to formulate those ideas and now they have them on paper bound for Rome. Numerous colleagues reviewed portions of the manuscript and offered valuable suggestions and encouragement. Toward the end of this research project I read Eli Saslow's book *Ten Letters* (2011), and knew I had a winner. His volume recounts the importance of letters sent to President Barak Obama by ordinary citizens like yourself. Yes, letters got through to the most powerful person in the world. He read some of them and the citizen opinions had an impact on public policy. Despite all my previous doubts, I am convinced this project was a good idea and back in 2007 I really was on the right track.

Many thanks are in order to the support staff of Trafford Publishing for their email reminders that deadlines have to be met. Kudos to those who granted permission to reprint various articles. Finally, I thank my wife, Norma, and our two children, Jonathan and Danielle. You are my inspiration and please keep it up. Mere words cannot express the importance of your love and support.

Rochester, Michigan, October, 2011.

INTRODUCTION

How does the average person get through to one of the most isolated public figures in the history of the modern world? No pope in the last 25 years has ever held a press conference as we understand the term. Obviously interviews on EWTN (Mother Angelica's Catholic TV station) do not qualify. Popes do not, on a regular basis, take or answer questions from a wide variety of journalists and Christian leaders about Catholic issues and problems. The current pope has never explained himself with follow up questions to the general public regarding his stand on women in the church, his role in Germany's priest sexual abuse crisis while he was Archbishop, or his stand on married priests. Some have rightly described Benedict's trips to the U.S. and Australia as papal pep rallies "designed to cheer the team during hard times."[1]

To counteract this closed organizational style, I have asked college students (about 10 % of whom were older and non-traditional students) to write Pope Benedict XVI a letter and tell him what they think. Are things ok? . . . . Are there problems which they feel need fixing? Maybe he will listen to them, I thought, although he failed to acknowledge or listen to those who have questioned his recent policies or pronouncements.[2] Simply put, students were invited over a three-year period (2007-2010) to contribute a letter to a book I was assembling called, *Letters to Pope Benedict.* They were

---

[1]   Suzanne Sataline, "Pontiff's Visit Seen as Rally for church beset by problems," *The Wall Street Journal*, April 14, 2008, p. A3.

[2]   Award winning author, Garry Wills, says that his ideas are simply ignored by Catholic church leaders. For five years Benedict ignored Cardinals and bishops who asked him to change his policy of "no condoms to prevent AIDS."

free to say whatever they wanted. Some used pseudonyms to protect their job status. In effect, I was turning the tables on this modern apostle—St. Paul wrote letters to his early Christian churches to teach them how to live a Christian life. Now these college students are writing letters to the modern apostle and leader of the Roman Catholic church (1.1 billion members) and offering their views on the Catholic church. From the type of letters in this volume one can see that a wide variety of opinions and perspectives exist in and outside the Catholic church. Students were free to write their own stories and they did. Only minor editing was done to make clear what students were trying to say. Letters that I felt unfairly attacked the Pope or the Catholic church were eliminated. After reading what these 34 students had to say, I decided to help the reader of this volume recall some of the controversial issues referred to in the letters. Hence, there are newspaper articles and notes interspersed throughout the book. It is clear that these epistles are for the pope to read and ponder, but this project is for everybody to listen, to learn, and to react. People should know what others are saying about the pope and the Catholic church. These notes from college students can give Vatican decision-makers pause for thought—are we on the right track? Are we building a bridge to nowhere?

Will the pope ignore the views of these college students I have met over the years as they bring their concerns to him? Only time will tell.

R. John Kinkel, Oakland University, Rochester, Michigan, September, 2011.

THE LETTERS

I. TIMES HAVE CHANGED.

Dear Pope Benedict:

The Roman Catholic Church is one of the largest religious denominations in the world and I respect it a lot. However, one of my major concerns is the fact that the younger generation is not attending church on a regular basis. The Catholic Church has not done a good job in drawing the younger generation into the fold. Times have changed and tradition is not a high priority for young people. I believe you must move away from some traditions and find new ways of getting your message out.

Adina Derecichei
Madison Heights, Michigan, December 2007

II. REFORM IS NEEDED.

Dear Pope Benedict:

The hour has arrived for change and reform. Gone are the days when we could sit back and let the hand play itself out. The fruit is now ripe for picking and the Papacy can no longer ignore the growing evidence that mass attendance on college campuses is way down and the decline in vocations to the priesthood is well documented. The answers to these problems rest on the same plane of opportunity: the college campus. It is here that religion is explored more personally and developed in a way that is quite different from when we were living in our parents' house. For here more than anywhere else, young people make decisions about their lifestyle that they will carry with them for the rest of their lives. The fact that church attendance among the college demographic is low, does not bode well for church leaders looking for young men to join the priesthood. The general consensus regarding this problem is that the church is no longer meeting the needs of its congregation.

The fundamental problem is in the church service. While I am aware that it is the church's tendency to adhere to ancient tradition, it is becoming an issue of more concern with significant consequences if not addressed thoroughly and quickly. For many students like me searching for our own path of spirituality, it is discouraging to attend liturgy services which appear to be putting the main emphasis on the ritual rather than the message. College students like myself like to believe that something has changed from the time I started going to mass as an infant with my family to now when I am responsible for my own attendance. Haven't we matured enough to hear a new message, or experience the revitalization of the church? College students are in a transition period where we are realizing there is more to our routine than studying, eating, sleeping, and partying. There is something missing, but we are afraid to admit it.

It is in this regard that the Church can provide a solution, but officials must change their routine because it is no longer effective on the college campus. Many of us may believe that since we may not have the healthiest and most moral lifestyle, it would be hypocritical for us to attend a place where everyone on the surface seems perfect. History illustrated the fact that when the church service was converted into the vernacular, the church prospered and provided generously for its congregation. We ask you to make the message much clearer for us, for being on our own, sometimes the message and guidance of our parents is lost or unavailable to us.

It is time to shed the misconception that priests are there to condemn the student for their lifestyle from the pulpit. If this goal is ever to be realized, then perhaps there won't be such difference between attendance at the Christmas masses and regular masses. Furthermore, the more we see ourselves in the priest, the more likely we can see ourselves as the priest, and increase vocations. It is time to break the barrier between church and college, but this can only be realized through satisfying communication.

Sincerely,
Josh Buchanan, Miami University, Oxford, Ohio, 2007

III. GIVE GAYS A BREAK

Dear Pope Benedict:

   I was raised a Catholic and attended Catholic schools through high school. I have always been a supporter of the Catholic faith and its beliefs regarding various social issues. However, I am a firm believer in giving homosexuals the right to wed in holy matrimony if they choose to do so. I was taught that God is a loving God and accepts all who come to Him as sinners seeking forgiveness. Doesn't He love all people? Homosexuals, whether they have freely chosen their sexual lifestyle or believe they are born with this orientation, need to be treated fairly by the church. Everyone is a sinner and needs to be forgiven for what they have done. Homosexuals should not be excluded from the church because of their different sexual needs. I have grown up and attended school with people who came out of the closet and admitted they were gay. That should not mean that God loves them less or that they are less holy. We are all equal in God's eyes and this equality should be extended to gays if they wish to marry. Love does not have a special color or gender and the church should treat all as equals. For a religion with such a rich history, it would be a shame for members to exit the church when all are supposed to be welcomed and treated with dignity. The practice of religion is one of the most intimate relationships we have, and everyone, homosexuals included, should not be condemned for their actions.

                              Alysse Miller, Royal Oak, Michigan, 2007

[What is she talking about? The article below helps to explain the problem]

Pope says gay unions are false
Sees a weakening of marriage
By Michael Paulson, Boston Globe Staff | June 7, 2005

Pope Benedict XVI, offering his first detailed critique of gay unions since his elevation to the pontificate six weeks ago, yesterday described same-sex marriages as "pseudo-matrimony."

In a speech to a conference on families held by the Diocese of Rome, Benedict made clear in strong language that he intends to pursue the hard-line defense of traditional Catholic teachings that made him controversial in his role as Pope John Paul II's chief enforcer of church doctrine.

"The various forms of the dissolution of matrimony today, like free unions, trial marriages and going up to pseudo-matrimonies by people of the same sex, are rather expressions of an anarchic freedom that wrongly passes for true freedom of man," he said, speaking at the Basilica of St. John Lateran in Rome.

The pope also criticized divorce and artificial contraception in his speech, in which he referred to "banalization of the human body" and said "the greatest expression of freedom is not the search for pleasure," according to the Reuters news agency.

Benedict made his remarks at a time when same-sex marriage has become a hotly contested public policy issue in Western societies. Same-sex marriage was legalized in Massachusetts last year, although the Legislature is still deciding whether to put on the ballot a measure banning gay marriage, and same-sex unions are legal in Vermont and Connecticut. Same-sex marriage is legal in Belgium, the Netherlands, and parts of Canada, and Spain has been moving toward legalization.

But the development has sparked resistance, especially in the United States, where many states have passed laws or constitutional amendments prohibiting same-sex marriage. Most recently, the California Legislature defeated a measure legalizing same-sex marriage.

Before he became pope, Benedict—then Cardinal Joseph Ratzinger—was the primary explainer of Pope John Paul II's oft-stated opposition to same-sex marriage. In 2003, Ratzinger wrote an important Vatican document outlining the church's opposition to same-sex marriage; the document became controversial because of its assertion that "Allowing children to be adopted by persons living in such unions would actually mean doing violence to these children, in the sense that their condition of dependency would be used to place them in an environment that is not conducive to their full human development."

Benedict's opposition to homosexuality is longstanding. In 1986, Ratzinger signed another doctrinal document declaring that "It is only in the marital relationship that the use of the sexual faculty can be morally good. A person engaging in homosexual behavior therefore acts immorally."

"This does not mean that homosexual persons are not often generous and giving of themselves," he wrote then, "but when they engage in homosexual activity they confirm within themselves a disordered sexual inclination which is essentially self-indulgent."

Benedict has spoken frequently about his concern that there is no absolute sense of right and wrong in modern society. On April 18, before the conclave at which he was elected pope, he warned that "We are building a dictatorship of relativism that does not recognize anything as definitive and whose ultimate goal consists solely of one's own ego and desires."

Since his election, the pope has spoken only a few times about political matters; last week he declared his support for an effort by the Italian bishops to persuade voters to boycott a referendum that would overturn a law restricting fertility treatments.

Scholars said Benedict's remarks yesterday were unsurprising, but serve as a reminder that the direct language and doctrinal orthodoxy for which he has been known are not likely to change.

"This is blunt, but it's intentional," said Chester Gillis, chairman of the theology department at Georgetown University. "He's not a man who speaks idly or without preparation. He wants a sharp demarcation between Christian values and what contemporary culture might condone—there's a sharp line and he wants to make that clear."

Gillis said Benedict's remarks fit in, not only with his critique of homosexual relationships, but also with his expressed concerns about contemporary culture, which he views as overly secular.

"This is confirming what everybody knew about this pope," Gillis said.

A former student of Benedict said the pope's description of same-sex marriages as an expression of "anarchic freedom" refers to a contemporary philosophy that "we can do whatever we wish." Benedict believes instead in a form of human freedom that is limited by God's will, according to the scholar, the Rev. Joseph Fessio.

"This is not a surprise—you'll find this statement in the catechism of the Catholic Church and everywhere you look for it in the whole 2,000-year history of the church," said Fessio, who founded Ignatius Press, which has published Benedict's works in the United States.

But gay rights advocates criticized the pope's remarks, as expected as they might have been.

"The comments by Pope Benedict XVI on gay civil marriage . . . sadly reflect what many had feared would be the continued language of hatred and disrespect that has come from the Vatican for many years towards gays and lesbians," said Charles Martel, a Catholic layman who serves on the board of the Religious Coalition for the Freedom to Marry, a Massachusetts organization. "The pope is creating a dangerous climate of inciting hatred towards gays and lesbians, and needs to be held accountable in attempting to encourage civil societies to perpetuate this prejudice."

And in Washington, Joe Solmonese, an Attleboro native who serves as president of the Human Rights Campaign, a gay rights advocacy organization, said in a statement, "It is unfortunate that the pope would choose so early in his pontificate to sweepingly condemn so many faithful Catholics. There is a long biblical tradition of showing love and compassion for all. It is from that tradition that so many fair-minded Catholics want to see their pope speaking."

Michael Paulson can be reached at mpaulson@globe.com.

IV. YOUR RELIGION IS GOOD.

Dear Pope Benedict:

I am not a Catholic and have no intention of changing what you think or what anyone else would think about your religion. The Catholic religion has been a pretty big influence in my life because most of the people in the society I grew up in (Kenya), belonged to the Catholic faith. One thing I noticed was that they were really dedicated in working together for a cause. They spent time together, even besides the meetings they had in church on Sundays.

If anyone needed any kind of help, e.g., money, food, the Catholics would get together and everyone helped to raise money according to their means. If someone was sick, then the doctor would treat them, and if they did not have the means to pay, the service would be free.

I would say your religion is very good and that people following the religion have always been a great help, not only to people like me, but the society as a whole.

> *Sincerely,*
> *Mr. Hardik Dave, Royal Oak, Michigan, December 2007*

V. EMBRACE RELIGIOUS TOLERANCE

Dear Pope Benedict:

I am not a very religious person. However, that is because I believe the Catholic church has too many restrictions and lacks tolerance. The Catholic church believes that homosexuals are sinners. I have many homosexual friends and I think a group, such as the Catholic church, should be promoting love for their fellow man and not hate based on sexual preference. There is not just intolerance for homosexuals in the church but negativism toward other religions as well. The Catholic church is allowed to believe what they want, so why should they be allowed to judge and condemn others for their beliefs? The Catholic church needs to create a more accepting attitude; it needs to change with society. How can a society base its beliefs on something created centuries ago? The world and the people in it are not the same as those living a thousand years ago and religion should not try to make it so. Try and promote tolerance and change for the future. You won't lose your followers; you'll only gain new ones.

Melanie Satoran, Miami University, Oxford, Ohio, 2007

VI. THE CATHOLIC CHURCH IS STRONG.

Dear Pope Benedict:

This is my first letter to a pope and I find it difficult to decide on what to include. However, this is what I feel needs to be said. I love the Catholic church and the fact that it is my church, it hurts me personally when I see that Catholicism is being attacked by national and international political forces. This pain has caused me to think a lot about the church and how it is handling current issues.

I believe you and other church leaders are handling everything rather well. The power of Catholicism is strongly based on tradition. These traditions have stayed firm throughout the years and centuries of our religion's history. If our church was to change these traditions, our religion would be weakened. Here in America there is much talk about the separation of church and state. This was originally designed mostly for the benefit of the state; however, I believe this separation can be used to help our church. The church needs to separate from the political world and focus on what I believe to be more important matters: the church members taking care of each other.

With all my heart, I strongly encourage you to further improve and strengthen Catholicism. Caring for the poor down the street and around the world is something Catholics do everyday. We give money at various church collections for them. We work at soup kitchens and even travel to third world countries for them. This is love. A second form of this Christian caring is education. Education needs to be continued as a keystone to Catholicism. I personally attended a Catholic high school and found it to be the most tightly-knit academic community I have ever experienced. The teachers, the Catholic brothers, and the students all cared for each other. And here in the field of education is where I think the church can work at increasing the number of young faithful. Religious education combined with its moral dimension appealed to me as a teen ager. Growing up in today's society I think one needs both—one alone is not enough. Using this combination, I fully believe that many young people will stay with the church and others will turn toward Catholicism.

These thoughts might seem insignificant to you, but I wanted you to know that this is my view of religion. When I go to church, I am not thinking of the Catholic church as a world power. I think of it as a community, and my role in it, the people around me and the Lord. This is how our religion started with emphasis on self, others, and the Holy Trinity. Focusing on this level of Catholicism, there is no controversy and no way to go wrong.

I sincerely thank you for your time in reading my letter and the other letters in this volume. Students like me want and need to have our voices heard and as a new pope we hope you listen to our opinions. We might be young and inexperienced, but that could be the key to an alternative point of view that you might consider.

God Bless you,
Thomas D. Seibert, Miami University, Oxford Ohio, 2007

VII. WHY NO WOMEN PRIESTS?

Dear Pope Benedict,

I have been baptized and raised Catholic. I grew up in a community that was highly populated by other Catholic families and I have attended mass with my family every Sunday for as far back as I can remember. Through my experiences I have observed how the Catholic Church provides a sense of belonging, comfort, and guidance in people's everyday lives. The Church's leading role in society has existed for hundreds of years and is still needed very much today. However, the fact that the Catholic Church relies so heavily upon its ancient teachings and traditions seems to be a growing problem in our world. In my opinion, some of the Catholic Church's teachings are outdated and should certainly be reconsidered by today's standards.

Being a modern day Catholic woman the ancient teaching that bothers me the most is the tradition that states no woman is to be ordained a priest. I understand that this idea was created many years ago when women were considered to be inferior to men; I find it extremely frustrating, however, that the Church still holds on to this belief. One of the great philosophers of the medieval Church, Thomas Aquinas once said,

"Woman is an occasional and incomplete being . . . a misbegotten male. It is unchangeable that woman is destined to live under man's influence and has no authority from her Lord" (Sum. Theol. 1, Q 92).

I find it quite funny how he says that women's destiny to live under men is unchangeable. On the contrary I believe that the growing success of the independent woman today would highly contradict that statement. Times have changed quite *a bit since the 13th century when Thomas Aquinas was around, which leads me to my next question, why has the Church not changed as well?*

A Bible passage from the New Testament enforces the equality of women in the early Catholic Church:

"There is neither Jew nor Greek, there is neither slave nor free person, there is not male and female; for you are all one in Christ Jesus" (Gal 3:28).

Also seen in the New Testament is a less than appealing statement about women by St. Paul:

"A Man . . . is the glory of but God; but woman is the glory of man. For man was not made from woman, but woman from man. Neither was man created for women, but women for man (1 Corinthians 11:7-9)."

Obviously the Church today would no longer agree with this immoral statement, so why would it support a rule that is very much so morally degrading toward women?

Jesus Christ was a firm believer in the equality of all people, and believed that everyone deserved respect, particularly women. Jesus broke cultural taboos; in the Bible he is seen teaching women and giving them the right to discuss the Torah, even though such dialogue was forbidden by the Jewish law of their society. He spoke freely to them in public and performed miracles for them and on them, even though they were seen as "lowly creatures" in those days. In several of his stories Jesus showed concern for females; take for example the "Parable of the Woman and the Lost Coin" (Luke 15:8) and the "Parable of the Persistent Widow." He was friends with women and a number of them made up his closest followers. Jesus gave women the respect they deserved in a time when this was considered highly unacceptable, so again I question why the Catholic Church does not model itself after Jesus' teachings, and treat women with equal privileges. For as long as I have been old enough to understand this concept, I have been confused and disappointed as to why the Catholic Church still relies on a degrading tradition that was established hundreds of years ago.

I believe the Roman Catholic Church needs to get its head out of the history books, and catch up with society. The number of first year college students with no religious affiliation has nearly doubled in the past thirty years. This fact alone shows that times are changing very quickly. An increasing number of people are beginning to seek spiritual development outside of established religious organizations. People want the guidance and comfort of religion without all the strict rules and guidelines and if the Catholic Church remains steadfast in old tradition, it may lose the support of a new, ambitious generation.

Erika Bussard,
Miami University, Oxford Ohio, First-Year Student 2007

R. John Kinkel, Ph.D.

ᵀᵉˡᵉᵍʳᵃᵖʰ.co.uk | Print version

Pope says Vatican will excommunicate women priests

By Our Foreign Staff
Last updated: 2:50 AM BST 30/05/2008

The Vatican has issued its most explicit decree so far against the ordination of women priests, vowing to punish them and the bishops who ordain them with automatic excommunication.

The decree, published in the Vatican newspaper L'Osservatore Romano, makes the Church's existing ban on women priests more explicit by clarifying that excommunication would follow all such ordinations.

People excommunicated from the Catholic Church are forbidden from receiving the sacraments or sharing in acts of public worship.

Rev. Tom Reese, a senior fellow at the Woodstock Theological Center at Georgetown University, said he thought the decree was meant to send a warning to the growing number of Catholics who favour admitting women to the priesthood.

"I think the reason they're doing this is that they've realised there is more and more support among Catholics for ordaining women, and they want to make clear that this is a no-no," Mr Reese said.

The Church says it cannot change the rules banning women from the priesthood because Christ chose only men as his apostles. Catholic law states that only a baptised male can be made a priest.

But advocates of women's ordination say Christ was only acting according to the social norms of his time.

They cite the letters of Saint Paul, some of the earliest texts of Christianity, to show that women played important roles in the early church.

VIII. PREACH RELIGIOUS UNDERSTANDING.

Dear Pope Benedict:

In the past few years the papacy has changed its course from uniting Catholic leadership, to a policy that encourages division. A common cause for peace between Catholics, Muslims, Jews and Protestants all over the world exists and must be nurtured. This common cause is in the interest of all humanity. We should find a common, uniting force that binds us together instead of throwing obstacles in the path of friendship. A pope that calls Protestant denominations "defective" and "not real churches" and then provokes division between Christians and Islam (Regensburg speech) is not needed in our modern world. Our world needs leaders who promote respect and dignity toward all, and not finger pointing. As we move to my generation's future, please remember we must find a common ground or we will destroy the ground we stand on.

Peter Young
Royal Oak, Michigan
December, 2007

IX. WORK TOWARD GENUINE UNITY.

Dear Pope Benedict XVI:

Your predecessors have sought to unify the people of God in one Catholic Church under Papal authority. Jesus prayed for unity among us (John 17:21), and so unity is a good thing. However, it is the assertion of monarchical, universal authority by you and your predecessors that I question. The assertion of Papal authority regarding the filioque issue divided the church in 1054 A.D. Such a change in the Nicene Creed should only have been made via an ecumenical council of the church. A few centuries later, Martin Luther sought to reform the Church but to no avail. His concerns were met with a Papal demand that he recant, and an unspoken, "or else". The result was to further fracture the Church. Other valid issues are now pressing upon the Church, such as the role of women and the marriage of priests. Inaction on these issues is causing many to leave the Church.

Jesus said, ". . . you are Peter, and on this rock I will build my church . . ." (Matt 16:18), and he gave Peter "the keys of the kingdom of heaven" and authority to "bind and loose". The real rock was Peter confessing the truth of who Jesus was, not Peter himself. Will you acknowledge that? A few verses later when Peter opposed Jesus, he was told, "Get behind me, Satan! You are a stumbling block to me". This stumbling block also meant a rock, and showed that Peter himself was not stable like a rock. Two chapters later, Jesus gave the other disciples the authority to "bind and loose" (Matt 18:18). More generally, the Apostle Paul wrote that we are ". . . built on the foundation of the apostles and prophets, with Christ Jesus himself as the chief cornerstone" (Ephesians 2:19-20). The emphasis here is on Christ, not Peter. Furthermore,

Peter wrote to us all: "as you come to him, the living Stone—rejected by men but chosen by God and precious to him—you also, like living stones, are being built into a spiritual house to be a holy priesthood . . ." (1 Peter 2:4-5). So, all of us (male and female, Gal 3:28), are living stones, construction materials for the household of God, priests who can share the keys of the kingdom with others. We all have spiritual gifts for building the spiritual house (1 Cor 12), and we will not permit you to suppress them, as was mostly done in the past. Our chief cornerstone is Christ himself, not you as his representative.

Can we work toward unity? Yes, but it will not be under your authority, which has divided us and continues to do so as long as you claim to be more than you rightly are. Recent experience with sexual abuse by priests suggests that you and your fellow bishops are incapable of real change without external force. Therefore, the unity we hope for is by growing ties between individual Christians and between denominations, basically independently of you. Our hoped-for unity is no longer that of the Catholic Church, but rather that of the catholic, universal church. Will you join us? What are you willing to do for the sake of unity?

Sincerely,
Dale L. Partin (A Protestant Brother), Ray, Michigan

AP Associated Press **Pope: Other Christians not true churches**

By Nicole Winfield, Associated Press Writer | July 10, 2007

LORENZAGO DI CADORE, Italy—Pope Benedict XVI reasserted the primacy of the Roman Catholic Church, approving a document released Tuesday that says other Christian communities are either defective or not true churches and Catholicism provides the only true path to salvation.

The statement brought swift criticism from Protestant leaders. "It makes us question whether we are indeed praying together for Christian unity," said the World Alliance of Reformed Churches, a fellowship of 75 million Protestants in more than 100 countries.

"It makes us question the seriousness with which the Roman Catholic Church takes its dialogues with the reformed family and other families of the church," the group said in a letter charging that the document took ecumenical dialogue back to the era before the Second Vatican Council.

It was the second time in a week that Benedict has corrected what he says are erroneous interpretations of the Second Vatican Council, the 1962-1965 meetings that modernized the church. On Saturday, Benedict revived the old Latin Mass—a move cheered by Catholic traditionalists but criticized by more liberal ones as a step backward from Vatican II.

Among the council's key developments were its ecumenical outreach and the development of the New Mass in the vernacular, which essentially replaced the old Latin Mass.

Benedict, who attended Vatican II as a young theologian, has long complained about what he considers its erroneous interpretation by liberals, saying it was not a break from the past but rather a renewal of church tradition.

The Congregation for the Doctrine of the Faith, which Benedict headed before becoming pope, said it was issuing the new document Tuesday because some contemporary theological interpretations of Vatican II's ecumenical intent had been "erroneous or ambiguous" and had prompted confusion and doubt.

The new document—formulated as five questions and answers—restates key sections of a 2000 text the pope wrote when he was prefect of the congregation, "Dominus Iesus," which riled Protestant and other Christian denominations because it said they were not true churches but merely ecclesial communities and therefore did not have the "means of salvation."

The commentary repeated church teaching that says the Catholic Church "has the fullness of the means of salvation."

"Christ 'established here on earth' only one church," said the document released as the pope vacations at a villa in Lorenzago di Cadore, in Italy's Dolomite mountains.

The other communities "cannot be called 'churches' in the proper sense" because they do not have apostolic succession—the ability to trace their bishops back to Christ's original apostles—and therefore their priestly ordinations are not valid, it said.

The Rev. Sara MacVane, of the Anglican Centre in Rome, said that although the document contains nothing new, "I don't know what motivated it at this time."

"But it's important always to point out that there's the official position and there's the huge amount of friendship and fellowship and worshipping together that goes on at all levels, certainly between Anglicans and Catholics and all the other groups and Catholics," she said.

The document said that Orthodox churches were indeed "churches" because they have apostolic succession and enjoyed "many elements of sanctification and of truth." But it said they do not recognize the primacy of the pope—a defect, or a "wound" that harmed them, it said.

"This is obviously not compatible with the doctrine of primacy which, according to the Catholic faith, is an 'internal constitutive principle' of the very existence of a particular church," said a commentary from the congregation that accompanied the text.

Despite the harsh tone, the document stressed that Benedict remains committed to ecumenical dialogue.

"However, if such dialogue is to be truly constructive it must involve not just the mutual openness of the participants, but also fidelity to the identity of the Catholic faith," the commentary said.

The top Protestant cleric in Benedict's homeland, Germany, complained the Vatican apparently did not consider that "mutual respect for the church status" was required for any ecumenical progress.

In a statement titled "Lost Chance," Lutheran Bishop Wolfgang Huber argued that "it would also be completely sufficient if it were to be said that the reforming churches are 'not churches in the sense required here' or that they are 'churches of another type'—but none of these bridges is used" in the Vatican document.

The Vatican statement, signed by the congregation prefect, American Cardinal William Levada, was approved by Benedict on June 29, the feast of Saints Peter and Paul—a major ecumenical feast day.

There was no indication why the pope felt it necessary to release it now, particularly since his 2000 document summed up the same principles.

Some analysts suggested it could be a question of internal church politics or that the congregation was sending a message to certain theologians it did not want to single out. Or, it could be an indication of Benedict using his office as pope to again stress key doctrinal issues from his time at the congregation.

In fact, the only theologian cited by name in the document for having spawned erroneous interpretations of ecumenism was Leonardo Boff, a Brazilian clergyman who left the priesthood and was a target of then Cardinal Joseph Ratzinger's crackdown on liberation theology in the 1980s. ■

Remarks by Pope Benedict XVI in a speech in Germany have provoked outrage in the Muslim world and led to demands that the pontiff apologize for "insulting" Islam.

Below are some key excerpts from the Pope's speech at the University of Regensburg, entitled Faith, Reason and the University: Memories and Reflections.

ON UNIVERSITY LIFE

It is a moving experience for me to be back again in the university and to be able once again to give a lecture at this podium.

The university [of Bonn, where the Pope taught for a period from 1959] was also very proud of its two theological faculties. This profound sense of coherence within the universe of reason was not troubled, even when it was once reported that a colleague had said there was something odd about our university—it had two faculties devoted to something that did not exist: God.

That even in the face of such radical scepticism it is still necessary and reasonable to raise the question of God through the use of reason, and to do so in the context of the tradition of the Christian faith: this, within the university as a whole, was accepted without question.

ON HOLY WAR

I was reminded of all this recently, when I read . . . of part of the dialogue carried on—perhaps in 1391 in the winter barracks near Ankara—by the erudite Byzantine Emperor Manuel II Paleologus and an educated Persian on the subject of Christianity and Islam, and the truth of both.

In the seventh conversation . . . the emperor touches on the theme of the holy war. Without descending to details, such as the difference in treatment accorded to those who have the "Book" and the "infidels", he addresses his interlocutor with a startling brusqueness on the central question about the relationship between religion and violence in general, saying: "Show me just what Muhammad brought that was new, and there you will find things only evil and inhuman, such as his command to spread by the sword the faith he preached."

The emperor, after having expressed himself so forcefully, goes on to explain in detail the reasons why spreading the faith through violence is something unreasonable. Violence is incompatible with the nature of God and the nature of the soul. "God," he says, "is not pleased by blood—and not acting reasonably is contrary to God's nature. Faith is born of the soul, not the body. Whoever would lead someone to faith needs the ability to speak well and to reason properly, without violence and threats."

ON RELIGION AND REASON

The decisive statement in this argument against violent conversion is this: not to act in accordance with reason is contrary to God's nature. The editor, Theodore Khoury, observes: For the emperor, as a Byzantine shaped by Greek philosophy, this statement is self-evident. But for Muslim teaching, God is absolutely transcendent. His will is not bound up with any of our categories, even that of rationality.

At this point, as far as understanding of God and thus the concrete practice of religion is concerned, we are faced with an unavoidable dilemma. Is the conviction that acting unreasonably contradicts God's nature merely a Greek idea, or is it always and intrinsically true?

ON THEOLOGY AND SCIENCE

The liberal theology of the 19th and 20th Centuries ushered in a second stage in the process of dehellenisation, with Adolf von Harnack as its outstanding representative.

The intention here is . . . of broadening our concept of reason . . . Only thus do we become capable of that genuine dialogue of cultures and religions so urgently needed today.
Pope Benedict XVI

Jesus was said to have put an end to worship in favour of morality. In the end he was presented as the father of a humanitarian moral message.

Fundamentally, Harnack's goal was to bring Christianity back into harmony with modern reason.

[But] . . . any attempt to maintain theology's claim to be "scientific" would end up reducing Christianity to a mere fragment of its former self . . . This is a dangerous state of affairs for humanity, as we see from the disturbing pathologies of religion and reason which necessarily erupt when reason is so reduced that . . . religion or ethics no longer concern it.

CONCLUSION

The intention here is not one of retrenchment or negative criticism, but of broadening our concept of reason and its application . . . Only thus do we become capable of that genuine dialogue of cultures and religions so urgently needed today.

In the Western world it is widely held that only positivistic reason and the forms of philosophy based on it are universally valid. Yet the world's profoundly religious cultures see this exclusion of the divine from the universality of reason as an attack on their most profound convictions. A reason which is deaf to the divine and which relegates religion into the realm of subcultures is incapable of entering into the dialogue of cultures.

Story from BBC NEWS:
http://news.bbc.co.uk/go/pr/fr/-/2/hi/europe/5348456.stm

Published: 2006/09/15 10:37:32 GMT
© BBC MMVIII

X. HUMILITY IS A VIRTUE

Dear Pope Benedict:

The public apology of your predecessor, John Paul II, to the Greek Orthodox church (2001) is to me one of the most profound gestures of reconciliation by the Roman Catholic church since Vatican II. It raised the hopes of millions that the Church would move forward in clarifying its doctrine of truth and responsibility (infallibility). If the head of the Catholic church could admit its past errors in such a public way, it becomes an example to all governments on how to approach reconciliation.

I am concerned that your administration will turn away from that visionary stance, and return to what was, at best, a defensive, non-responsive stone walling on major church issues before Vatican II. Today, we need to see more humility and less self-righteousness.

Please follow the policies of your predecessor which will promote healing, reconciliation and justice through forgiveness not only of nations but of neighbors.

Sincerely,
Jon P. Grewer
Royal Oak, Michigan
December, 2007

XI. RETURN TO PRAYER RENEWAL.

Dear Pope Benedict:

I wish to thank you for representing the Catholic Church to the world. I am grateful to have a pope who I honor with much gratitude as the world evolves and struggles through desperate times. It is a gift from God to have such a holy man to turn to for support and prayer.

It is my deepest regret and concern that many Roman Catholics are not turning to their local churches for support through prayer and study with our religious leaders. I believe that Catholics need to be "ignited" once again to turn toward traditional prayer and guidance. I say this with respect to you and the Vatican itself. It is evident that our world is turning to other activities such as drugs, alcohol, and violence.

I ask that the Catholic Church recognize and act on the need for more faith experiences. The world needs the Lord more than anything else. You see, people need to know through the Catholic faith that the Lord = love, as you have stated so clearly in your encyclical "Deus Caritas est." That is the message the whole world needs. I believe, Your Holiness, you represent the message and the whole world respects and honors you even if you do not belong to their particular denomination. Please pray for us as we pray for you.

Shawn Bowery, 2007, Royal Oak, Michigan

XII. GOOD JOB, BUT CHANGE

Dear Pope Benedict:

The Catholic church is everywhere. In fact you have some of the biggest and most beautiful churches in the world. Even though I am impressed with the expansion of this religion, I have yet to understand why Catholics have not adapted to modern times. Life is ever-changing and so are people. Many things we used to believe in are no longer important. For example, some Catholics still believe that women are not equal to men, so why not have women more involved in your religion? After all, I think women have proven to be just as intelligent, efficient and Godly as men.

Yolie Morales, Royal Oak, Michigan, 2007

XIII. CHANGE OR THE CHURCH WILL DIE

Dear Pope Benedict:

I believe that the Catholic church is too strict and formal. Even though Catholicism is one of the oldest religions, it needs to make changes to accommodate our changing society. To not let gays be part of the denomination is ridiculous. God loves everybody no matter who they are as long as they believe and repent of their failings. Also, to not let women preach is sexist. Catholic ways need to change or many people will leave and form their own beliefs.

Veronica Grubba, Royal Oak, Michigan, 2007

XIV. THE GOOD, THE BAD, THE UGLY: CHANGE PLEASE

Dear Pope Benedict:

I would like to take this opportunity that my sociology professor, Dr. Kinkel, has provided, to write a letter on behalf of the Catholic parish. I am an alumnus of Miami University, Oxford, Ohio, with a bachelor of science in biochemistry and have been a member of the Catholic Church all of my life. Like many Catholics, I have likes and dislikes concerning the Catholic Church and its parishes across the world. In this day and age there has been great growth in the Catholic Church, mainly due to the traditional upbringing of individuals like myself, but many are dissatisfied with its bureaucratic style of leadership, the way the church has handled the sex abuse scandals, the dwindling numbers of priests, and the continued tradition that does not meet the needs of our youth. Our Church needs to listen to the parishioners and not ignore the words they speak. The parish wants to be satisfied and be filled with God's love and kindness.

Our Church needs to listen to all the people of the world. The Church must take the initiative in protecting our environment. We are all God's creations. I write to encourage our Catholic community to take the initiative in combating global warming, helping to fight AIDS in Africa, and supporting humanitarian relief in places such as Darfur. I write to encourage our Church to meet the needs of these people around the world.

God created the land, the oceans, and all the inhabitants on earth and it is therefore our duty to protect them. Global warming has become a great threat to our civilization and many have chosen to weigh the earth's ecosystems against the economy. Without the earth's vast resources, our economy would be nonexistent. The greatest solution to this planetary crisis is a moral response. Increased warming can be stopped, but only at the cost of our familiar ways of life. Our own population, for example, is at great risk. The world's population grew slowly at the beginning of time and now it has reached exponential growth, rapidly approaching the earth's limit. This limit is the maximum stress our earth can sustain. At this limit, our earth will be under great strain and our planetary ecosystems will be struggling to survive.

We must limit our population growth and I urge the Catholic Church to reconsider their stance on birth control. One of the greatest population problems we face is in the poorest continents such as Africa. This is the same place where AIDS is killing millions. Infant mortality is extremely high due to the lack of clean water, infectious disease, and the lack of proper nutrition. Education about birth control and the use of condoms to protect against infectious diseases (AIDS) and unwanted births will assist in solving some of these humanitarian crises in Africa. The practice of abstinence is an idealized solution to this situation, but unfortunately women have little power in Africa. They are submissive to the men and have little education regarding birth control. Abstinence may be a partial solution but condoms must also be utilized to promote public health. The Catholic Church needs to support causes that fight the spread of AIDS and global warming as well as other humanitarian crises around the world.

Women have an important role in Africa as well as across the globe and in the Catholic Church. The Catholic Church needs to support women and give them the opportunity to be ordained as priests. The Catholic Church can be improved by increasing the number of priests through removing restrictions on who can be priests. Women are very influential and can have a powerful impact on the Catholic community. The Catholic Church has ignored these women, who compose half of the world's population. It took a long time before women gained the right to vote, long after African Americans gained their freedom from slavery in the United States. Let's not let it take longer for women to be priests in the Catholic Church.

Celibacy among priests should be optional. This would increase the number of priests in the Catholic Church by great numbers, and eliminate many problems by adding new blood to the ministry. Deacons, for example, are married and have most of the training necessary to become priests. Many of these deacons are willing to become priests, but traditional Catholic law forbids it. Research has also found that men live healthier lives when they are with a companion such as a wife. The Catholic Church needs to do what is best for its community. Following tradition is not always the way to go.

Finally, I would like to comment upon divorce. I feel that it is unfortunate that the Catholic Church seems to imply that people will go to hell if they divorce and remarry. This is absolute nonsense. I know, coming from a divorced family, that people make wrong decisions in life that can cause great harm to family and friends. Much of this harm can never be repaired with both spouses living in the home. I feel that my parents' divorce was for the best and has drawn me closer to my parents. I have learned from their mistakes as adults and most of all I have learned to forgive them. I would be a different person to this day if my parents were not divorced. It changes everyone around you, not just yourself. But the most important point that I want to make is that sometimes, certain people cannot prevent disasters from occurring. In these cases, people should not be punished. My mother, for example, did nothing wrong, and yet she has refused to go to any Catholic service because she is not allowed to take communion which fact demoralizes her and destroys her respect for the church. The Catholic community loses a great number of wonderful people because the church maintains many traditional views that harm people. It is time to change.

Our Catholic Church is afraid to change tradition in an ever changing world. I have grown up and still consider myself a young Catholic and it amazes me that throughout history the church has not changed many of its traditional ways. As a parish we are forced to play the game or leave the church. We need to reorient ourselves about the Gospel and be innovators in the world today; we should strive to change the bureaucratic government that the Catholic Church has become. Great scholars such as Gregor Mendel, Roger Bacon, Galileo Galilei, Vesalius, Cauchy, Lavoisier, and many more from our church have contributed to science, math, and astronomy, etc. Many were not accepted because they broke from tradition. But now they are hailed as great thinkers and philosophers in our modern society. Our Church is deeply rooted in history but it is time to break from some of its traditions and enter into an age of growth and prosperity. The future holds great things for the Catholic Church if we dare to reach for it.

With love,
Christopher Ruark Miami University, Oxford, Ohio, 2007

BBC NEWS

Pope rejects condoms for Africa

The spread of HIV and Aids in Africa should be tackled through fidelity and abstinence and not by condoms, Pope Benedict XVI has said.

Speaking to African bishops at the Vatican, the Pope described HIV/Aids in Africa as a "cruel epidemic".

But he told them: "The traditional teaching of the church has proven to be the only failsafe way to prevent the spread of HIV/Aids."

More than 60% of the world's 40m people with HIV live in sub-Saharan Africa.

In South Africa alone, 600-1,000 people are thought to die every day because of Aids.

Pope Benedict, who was elected to succeed John Paul II in April, has already signalled that he will maintain a strictly traditional line on issues including abortion and homosexuality.

Before being elected pope, Benedict served as head of the Vatican's doctrinal office.

These were his first public comments on the issue of Aids/HIV and contraception since taking office.

It is of great concern that the fabric of African life, its very source of hope and stability, is threatened by divorce, abortion, prostitution, human trafficking and a contraception mentality.
Pope Benedict

He was addressing bishops from South Africa, Botswana, Swaziland, Namibia and Lesotho, who had travelled to the Vatican for a routine papal audience.

Some Catholic clergymen have argued that the use of condoms to stem the spread of the disease would be a "lesser of two evils".

The Pope warned that contraception was one of a host of trends contributing to a "breakdown in sexual morality", and church teachings should not be ignored.

"It is of great concern that the fabric of African life, its very source of hope and stability, is threatened by divorce, abortion, prostitution, human trafficking and a contraception mentality," he added.

The virus "seriously threatens the economic and social stability of the continent," the Pope said.

The UN estimates that without new initiatives and greater access to drugs, more than 80 million Africans may die from Aids by 2025 and HIV infections could reach 90 million, or 10% of the continent's population.

Story from BBC NEWS:
http://news.bbc.co.uk/go/pr/fr/-/2/hi/europe/4081276.stm

Published: 2005/06/10 15:04:01 GMT
© BBC MMVIII

BBC NEWS

Pope 'distorting condom science'

One of the world's most prestigious medical journals, the Lancet, has accused Pope Benedict XVI of distorting science in his remarks on condom use.

It said the Pope's recent comments that condoms exacerbated the problem of HIV/Aids were wildly inaccurate and could have devastating consequences.

The Pope had said the "cruel epidemic" should be tackled through abstinence and fidelity rather than condom use.

A BBC correspondent says the Lancet's attack was unprecedentedly virulent.

Speaking during his first visit to Africa, the Pope said HIV/Aids was "a tragedy that cannot be overcome by money alone, that cannot be overcome through the distribution of condoms, which can even increase the problem".

The Pope said "the traditional teaching of the Church has proven to be the only failsafe way to prevent the spread of HIV/Aids".

The BBC's David Willey in Rome says the Church's view is that encouraging people to use condoms only minimises the effects of behaviour that in itself damages lives

'Devastating'

But the London-based Lancet said the Pope had "publicly distorted scientific evidence to promote Catholic doctrine on this issue".

It said the male latex condom was the single most efficient way to reduce the sexual transmission of HIV/Aids.

"Whether the Pope's error was due to ignorance or a deliberate attempt to manipulate science to support Catholic ideology is unclear," said the journal.

But it said the comment still stood and urged the Vatican to issue a retraction.

"When any influential person, be it a religious or political figure, makes a false scientific statement that could be devastating to the health of millions of people, they should retract or correct the public record," it said.

R. John Kinkel, Ph.D.

"Anything less from Pope Benedict would be an immense disservice to the public and health advocates, including many thousands of Catholics, who work tirelessly to try and prevent the spread of HIV/Aids worldwide."

Our correspondent says the article shows how far the Pope's attempts to justify the Vatican's position on condoms have misfired.

Story from BBC NEWS:
http://news.bbc.co.uk/go/pr/fr/-/2/hi/europe/7967173.stm

Published: 2009/03/27 01:06:07 GMT
© BBC MMX

> [Editor's note: In his new book *Light of the World* (2010), Pope Benedict stated that in certain circumstances Catholics can use condoms to prevent the spread of AIDS.]

XV. IM OUT, BUT YOU'RE OUT OF LINE

Dear Pope Benedict:

I have lost my faith. For many years, I had no desire to get it back either, and I was happy. Recently, like many other mid-twenty-somethings, I have started to wonder what happened to that faith, the starved, unimaginative, and immature faith that youth only allows. Committed to rediscovering a glimpse of this faith, I have read and reflected on religion more in the past year than I have in the past decade. Though I have not come near to finding faith, I have discovered that despite my Catholic education and upbringing—which frequently included mass not only once but twice a week—I can no longer call myself a Catholic, nor do I want to.

Growing up within the confines of the Church, I hardly knew of a world without it. My journeys through college and beyond have revealed so much that I did not know. For the first time, I have been exposed to individuals who challenge me and my faith, who are interested in my spiritual thoughts and opinions, and who encourage and respect my individuality rather than attempt to undo it. Unfortunately, you reject these good and compassionate people from the Church because of their homosexuality, their unwanted teen pregnancies, their drug use or some other doctrine du jour. How can a faith teach benevolence and selflessness while in the same breath cast these individuals aside, denying them their promised "salvation"?

And so I find myself wondering, why should I go back to this faith, why is it right for me? The truth is, the Church has given me no reason to believe that it is more deserving of my faith than any other religion. I find that to be the precise problem: no one seems to care about the individual. Everyone, on the other hand, seems to care a whole lot about you—the Pope, the Church, the Institution, the Tradition. I don't think that is what faith is meant to be, or what the apostles truly intended. I believe that faith is meant to be a personal journey of exploration, not a caravan down the beaten path. Either the Church must learn to rejoice in the individuality of its members, or suffer the loss of what could have been its most genuine supporters.

With that, I believe it is time for you to make a confession. Confess that you are human, just like the rest of us, and that you do not know all the answers. Confess that the strength of the Catholic Church lies in its community, and therein the strength of individuals' faith. Confess that individuals are not best nourished by tradition and certainty, but rather by expression and inquiry. Finally, Pope Benedict, confess that while extreme differences of belief and practice exist among you and your billion Catholics, you know that God will accept each and every one of us as we are, delighting in the myriad experiences, principles, teachings, and lives that separate us. It wouldn't hurt to further confess that while He is celebrating your differences, He's not likely shutting the door on mine.

I wish you well,
Sadie A. Breakstone, 2008, Detroit, Michigan

XVI. WORK ON RELIGIOUS UNDERSTANDING.

Dear Pope Benedict:

I was raised in a mixed religious household: my father is an Irish Catholic and my mother was born and raised Jewish. I was torn at a young age as to what religion was right for me. I attended a Catholic elementary school and took the lessons taught me by the nuns to heart. Treating others the way you wanted to be treated has become a personal motto, even though now I tend to follow many more of the Jewish traditions and beliefs.

I have been studying a lot of religious belief systems lately, and think that we are all interconnected . . . . that we all believe in the same God overall. The Jews, Christians, and followers of Islam worship the same God.

I think now is the time for us as a religious community to become more understanding of each other; we need to stop fighting over whose God is superior. I believe that if we all can stop this bickering, we could have a more tolerant society and accept each other.

> *Sincerely,*
> *Ashley Coates, Royal Oak, Michigan, 2008*

XVII. EXPECT YOU TO LEAD.

Dear Pope Benedict:

I don't want you to think I'm criticizing your contributions and hard work for Roman Catholics, but some things have to change. You should be more vocal with young people. The young people of today don't know the true values of the Catholic religion. It's like sitting in a classroom and the teacher is not present to teach. You are the leader and the voice. Tradition, values, and morals are important. You should let us as people and your followers know how you feel and let us know what we need to do to become better Catholics. If you need our help we will be there, but we need your help also. Please show us you care.

Sincerely,
Crystal Hussein, Dearborn, Michigan, February, 2008

XVIII. POSSIBLE CONVERT?

Dear Pope Benedict:

I have always been curious as to how the Catholic religion inspires an individual in the church. It appears to me as an outsider that the religion is steeped in older traditions. What I mean is that if you were not born Catholic, and you don't come from a long line of Catholics, how and why would a person wish to become a part of this religion. I am part of the out-group, but the religion has always held a bit of mystery to me. It seems to me that if you are not a part of the fold, there is no way in. How can an individual convert? I wish to be inspired . . . . how can this religion inspire me?

> *Sincerely,*
> *Monterasa Hughes, Royal Oak, Michigan, February, 2008*

XIX. WHY NOT INNOVATE?

Dear Pope Benedict:

I used to go to church every week, but not anymore. It's not that I don't care, but when I went to mass when I was young I was bored. Sitting there being talked at and preached to . . . . it aggravated me, as I know it does many people. I am concerned about two questions and hope you can help me understand. First why is prayer only in church on Sunday? Can we not broadcast sermons on TV and radio and pray from home? Will God not listen? Secondly, why has the church not done more to stay with its people? In modern times many people choose to believe nothing rather than you. You can stay true to your beliefs, and still change your sermon styles. Why no dancing and singing in church? No religious concerts? I've seen those work well, why don't you change?

Sincerely,
Martin Cook, Troy, Michigan, 2008

XX. MAINTAIN TRADITION OF CELIBACY?

Dear Pope Benedict,

There are so many problems in the world. People crave money and power and forget about their souls. You are one of the most influential persons in the world. With your words and actions, you are able to persuade people to change. You have to do everything that is in your power to help nations see that nothing good can come from evil.

I look at all religions with respect, but one issue that I have with the Catholic Church is the celibacy requirement for its priests. It should be optional. I think that would have to be changed one day for, it is illogical and it has brought a lot of grief to the church itself and to its members. The celibacy requirement for priests is absolutely outdated and detached from reality. How can a person who never had a family give advice to those who do?

There is no other religion in the world that demands celibacy from its ministers to my knowledge. History has shown that the celibacy requirement has and will lead to abuses in Churches. The latest chain of cases of priests abusing boys shows how dangerous this unrealistic requirement is. Because of these problems, many families have turned away from religion. The damage to the Church's image is enormous. The Church's financial losses are unspeakable.

However important traditions are, religion's survival may depend on the church's ability to adapt to times and be able to attract new followers. Canceling the celibacy requirement may be the only thing the Catholic Church can do to revitalize the church. Please be a leader who builds on tradition, but leads with vision.

Find a way to the hearts of people; make everything to turn them back to God, back to church, back to kindness, and love.

Sincerely,
Liliya Veysa, Royal Oak, Michigan, February, 2008

The Pope Confronts the Priest Sex Scandal

Pleased with the pontiff's response, victims now want the church to follow through

By Alex Kingsbury
Posted April 18, 2008, *U. S. News and World Report*

After years of near silence on the issue of the abuse and rape of children at the hands of pedophile priests, Pope Benedict XVI made public acknowledgement of the scandal a central theme of his first visit to the United States as head of the church. The first mention of the scandal came while still en route from Rome when he told reporters he was "deeply ashamed" about the scandal that had caused "great suffering."

It was the first time the papacy had directly addressed the victims of abusive clerics, and it signaled that Benedict's first trip to the United States as pontiff would be not just a state visit but an effort at reconciliation with American believers and an exercise in humility for the church's role in a scandal the pope conceded had been "very badly handled."

The allegations against Catholic priests first came to light in 2002 and have been an open wound for the church ever since, particularly in the cities of Boston and Los Angeles. All told there have been an estimated 13,000 victims and some 5,000 abusive priests since 1950. The church has paid a combined **$2 billion** in settlements to victims, most of which was paid in the past six years. Six dioceses around the country have been forced into bankruptcy because of abuse costs.

At an open-air mass inside a Washington, D.C., baseball stadium on Thursday, the pope again raised the traumatic legacy of the scandal. "I acknowledge the pain which the church in America has experienced as a result of the sexual abuse of minors," he told a crowd of 46,000 people. "No words of mine could describe the pain and harm inflicted by such abuse. It is important that those who have suffered be given loving pastoral attention. Nor can I adequately describe the damage that has occurred within the community of the church."

For some in attendance it was a fitting response to an issue that has cost the church dearly. "There is still a lot of hurt over the sexual abuse crisis in the church," said Maika Fowler before watching the pontiff deliver his homily. "He has really come to give his support to Catholics who feel discouraged by those kinds of issues in the church today and basically to say: 'I'm here with you, I feel for you, and things are going to get better.'"

The pope has addressed the scandal at nearly every public forum, including the mass in Washington and a meeting with a delegation of bishops.

In a surprise move, Benedict met privately on Thursday to pray with a group of victims. Boston Cardinal Sean O'Malley presented the pope with a book containing the names of 1,000 male and female victims of sexual abuse by members of the Boston archdiocese over the past few decades. "They prayed together. Also, each of them had their own individual time with the Holy Father," said a Vatican spokesman. "Some were in tears."

It was a moving moment, and one long in coming, say many Catholics. Yet while acknowledging that publicly addressing the issue was a good first step, victims and advocates called for greater transparency from the church as a follow-through to the pope's words.

"We've never before heard this type of honesty from the pope about what actually happened, and that's clearly a very encouraging sign—but talk is only as good as the actions that follow it up," said Dan Bartley, president of the Boston-based Voice of the Faithful, a group formed in the wake of the scandal to push for greater transparency and lay involvement in the management of the church. The group took out a full page advertisement in the *New York Times* in anticipation of the pope's visit calling for the pontiff to meet with victims of pedophilia and the removal of bishops responsible for covering up abuse or transferring known pedophiles within the ministry.

David Clohessy, director of the Survivors Network of those Abused by Priests, the country's largest such group, says that what's needed most are actions, like sanctioning bishops and others within the church who helped conceal and shuffle abusive priests to new parishes. "There's not a child on Earth who is any safer because of something the pope says; they will be safer because of what the pope does."

And abusive priests have not passed from the headlines. The day the pope was scheduled to arrive in New York City, a defrocked priest in New York was to be sentenced after pleading guilty to federal charges of enticing a minor for sex. The sentencing was later delayed, though prosecutors insisted it had nothing to do with the pontiff's visit. [*With Kent Garber and wire services*]

XXI. VERY IMPRESSED WITH CATHOLIC CHURCH.

Dear Pope Benedict:

I am a 41-year-old black man who was raised as a Baptist. Several years ago, I attended services at a Catholic church and continued to worship there 10 or 15 times over the course of a year or so. As someone who was raised as a Baptist, and had rarely been to the church service of any other denomination, I was pleasantly surprised by my experience with the Catholic church. In all honesty, I found the Catholic service to be very scripted and formal, in my opinion. Of course, maybe that was to be expected, considering that I was accustomed to the singing, preaching and shouting that is customary at most Baptist church services. My surprise came toward the end of the service, when communion began. I sat amazed at the sight of white, black, old, young, rich and poor people all drinking from the same cup that was being used to hold the wine that symbolized the blood of Christ. At all of the Baptist churches I had attended in the past everyone who took communion drank wine from individual glasses provided by the church. This particular Catholic church had a large contingent of homeless people and at the end of service parish members would provide them a meal free of charge. Through this experience I had with the Catholic church I got a better understanding of how God expects us to live. Jesus Christ preached love for your fellow man, empathy and compassion. He was not concerned about race or economic status. In that regard, I found the one, and thus far only, Catholic church that I have attended to be very Christ-like.

Roderick Mills, Royal Oak, Michigan, 2008

XXII. KEEP SOME TRADITIONS, CHANGE OTHERS.

Dear Pope Benedict,

I often hear my fellow college students complaining that the mass needs reform, and that traditions need to be changed in order to keep up with the modern world. I tend to differ from these students and enjoy the tradition that occurs during Mass. Everyday I see the commercial world attempting to appeal to a young audience with pop singers and athletes whose morals may be less than what one would hope. I believe that by changing the tradition of the Mass to appeal to a younger audience, you run the risk of falling into a commercial category, something that I am proud to say the Catholic religion has been able to avoid thus far. The purpose of the Mass is to have time to reflect with God and to witness the miracle that makes our religion unique.

I do, however, believe that there are some traditions in the church that are in need of modernization. Every year, all over the world, thousands die of AIDS. While this tragic disease has no cure, we know that there are many precautions that can be taken in order to prevent it. The use of condoms is among the most effective ways of preventing this disease, but unfortunately the Catholic church will not support the use of them, even among married couples. Is it not our duty as Catholics, as Christians, as human beings to preserve life in any way possible? It is my understanding that the church is against the use of condoms as contraception, but perhaps we need to consider the fact that they serve another purpose. Not only do they prevent the spread of AIDS from one adult to another, but they prevent the birth of children who will most likely be born infected with the disease themselves. And, who will be left to care for them when the disease claims the lives of their parents? The role of the Church in this situation is to provide people with the means to fight against this disease, not lead them to believe that they are sinning in their attempts to protect themselves and their children.

As an intelligent, independent and strong-willed woman, I believe that there is nothing in the world that I am less capable of doing because of my sex. As a child, I was often confused by the fact that there were no women priests. I was even more confused when I learned that the Church does not allow women to be priests (or deacons for that matter). I always thought of myself as lucky to be a woman since Jesus so obviously respected his mother and all other women he came in contact with. Why is it that while Jesus was the only one that would acknowledge the woman, we are one of the few Christian religions that will not recognize their ability to lead in our faith? Perhaps, then, it is not that we need to modernize in this area, but return to our original role as Christians, to follow Jesus and try in every way to live our lives as he would.

Along with this theme, I believe that priests should have the option to share their lives with Jesus, as well as a spouse. Priests are the ones that are supposed to set the example in the Church, and I believe that they are limited in their ability to do so when they cannot show an example of a good marriage. They are also limited in their ability to counsel on marriage when they have not experienced it themselves. I believe that in fully giving of yourself to another, you become closer to God than ever before. I do not believe that priests should be robbed of the privilege to love someone in such a way, and to express this love through marriage.

I appreciate the opportunity to be able to express my views and opinions about our wonderful faith to you. I hope that you consider the need for transformations within the Church, while still preserving that which is most important.

With Hope and Blessing,
Rebecca Johnson
Alexandria, VA

XXIII. SHOW US THE WAY.

Dear Pope Benedict,

I think the main point of Christianity is the 'love' which Jesus showed us by giving his life for the people. He was humiliated in order to understand our life, and he experienced all kinds of feelings like pain, love, joy . . . . same as we do. He showed us himself as the best example of the Christian life. He still listens to us, experiences the life we do, tells us, ... he lives with us. I want you to hear us, tell us clearly his will, so we can understand as Jesus showed us. Because we are all his daughters and sons who are equally expected to live our life as he taught us, please show us the way.

Ji Hee Kim, Royal Oak, Michigan, March, 2008

XXIV. EASE UP A BIT—TOO MANY RULES.

Dear Pope Benedict:

I think that the Catholic religion makes people very confused. The religion is so strict and has so many rules that some people don't understand it. I believe that Catholics shouldn't have to follow so many rules to be a part of their church. People need guidelines and something to believe in. That is why people select different religions and reject others. Catholics are too strict and spend too much time in church. People are busy and work long hours and so spending so much time in church can take way from important activities. I think this religion needs to ease up a little bit.

Sincerely, Tania Manitiu

Editor's note: While at church recently the Catholic priest told us out of the blue that he thought the church had too many rules. Apparently he felt this was one of the Church's problems. Here is the latest information on the New Code of Canon Law promulgated in 1983:[3]

> In 1959, Pope John XXIII (1958–1963) announced his desire to revise the *Code of Canon Law,* which had become slightly archaic in only 40 years. Before beginning the work of updating the laws of the Church, the pope saw the need to first summon and convene an ecumenical council. The Second Vatican Council met from 1962 through 1965 and issued 16 documents.

---

[3]   See the Code of Canon Law (Vatican, 1983).

It would take three more popes and another 20 years before the *Code of Canon Law* would finally be revised. After John XXIII came Paul VI (1963–1978), then John Paul I, who reigned for only a month and was succeeded by John Paul II in 1978.

Because reforms of Vatican II were well under way (including performing services in the common language of the congregation, ecumenical dialogue, and involvement of the laity) the canon laws of the Church needed to reflect not only the legal realities but the philosophy and theology that were behind them. The spirit of the law and the letter of the law needed to coincide and be known and applied by everyone.

Here's a summary of the changes made to the *Code of Canon Law* by the Second Vatican Council:

- **A reduction in the number of laws:** There are 1,752 canons in the 1983 *Code of Canon Law,* compared to the 1917 *Code of Canon Law,* which had 2,414 canons.

- **Despite these changes, church leaders in the 21st century argue that the new Code of Canon Law was inadequate for dealing with the priest sexual abuse crisis.**

- **No one at the Vatican has ever admitted failings in this regard.**

XXV. IMPROVE YOUTH CHURCH ATTENDANCE

Dear Pope Benedict:

I have a lot of respect for the Catholic religion. But one thing that I am concerned about is that the younger children do not have as much faith as people used to have many years ago. I believe there are several reasons why the church does not have as much influence on the younger generation as it did in the past. I believe that we can build faith and draw youth closer to God by having more masses made especially for the young children and making more interesting church events to attract children to attend church. The church can also have meetings for parents that would teach them how to bring their children closer to God.

Maisa Petros
Oakland Community College, 2008, Michigan

XXVI. THE CHURCH AND YOUTH.

Dear Pope Benedict:

I believe that today, young people are more concerned with watching television, having the best cars and dressing in fashionable clothes than attending church services and praying. I am surprised when I see these young people and how they have so little knowledge of God's way. Some do not know as much as they should about God and others do not even care to learn about God or church. In my opinion, we as a society can stop this from happening to our young children by encouraging the young children to attend church with their parents and that way they are going to be busy getting closer to God and not doing things that they should not be doing. We need to teach young children how to pray and to ask for forgiveness from God.

Mariam Petros
Oakland Community College, 2008, Royal Oak, Michigan

XXVII. JEWISH CHRISTIAN RELATIONS.

Dear Pope Benedict,

    For quite a while there have been many conflicts between Jewish and Catholic groups. Wars have even been fought over the seemingly insurmountable differences. What people fail to see are the similarities. Both Catholic and Jewish traditions have, to this day, excellent community service programs. Catholics and Jews take exceptional care of orphans, the elderly and anyone else, for that matter, who is in need of help. Many of these organizations are so caring that they are willing to help people who are from outside the faith. Such outstanding care for the unfortunate shows what is at the heart of these two religions. I point out these similarities to demonstrate that part of the core of these two religions is the values of compassion, care and lovingness.

    With these similarities in mind, I am forced to ask the question of why Jewish and Catholic relations have not been better throughout the years? It is clear that Christianity as a whole has improved attitudes toward Jews; the Catholic Church is one of the best examples of this. I am aware that in many cases the Church has gone out of the way to be accepting of other faiths, Judaism included, but I was wondering, if you, as Pope, think that any more can be done? Are there any more problems that still exist between Catholicism and Judaism?

    There are many sacred places that are considered holy to the Catholic Church in Israel. It has been proven by past acts of violence that holy sites can be targets of religious violence. Does the Church have any concern over protecting their relics in the Middle East? Regardless of what side you choose to be on it is clear that there is a lot of unneeded violence. The Church has a long history of being invested in that region of the world. Is there anything that the Church or the Pope can do in order to remedy the situations?

The time has come to stop looking at the past to emphasize differences between religions or cultures. One of the wonderful things about people is that we have the ability to change our views when the situation calls for it. It is clear this is what the Catholic Church has done when looking at other religions. No longer is there a need to condemn others for having different beliefs; we must learn to embrace people's religious differences. This is an active process, one that requires work from everybody involved. Hopefully the Catholic Church and you, the Pope, can continue to usher in such changes.

Jamie Schonberg, Oakland University, 2008

XXVIII. LOST GENERATION?

Dear Pope Benedict,

I believe the Roman Catholic Church is extremely important, and I am disappointed that the Catholic religion has not been able to keep the tradition of young families attending church on a regular basis. The way that people look at religious traditions today is completely different from the past. Especially for young people, attending church does not seem to be a top priority as it was for generations before. They seem to feel they could be doing better things with their time than sitting at church for Mass. Catholic churches need to reach out to the younger generation to attract them to attending church like their parents and grandparents once did. It is important that people keep in touch with their religious beliefs. This is why we need to make a change and attempt to get the younger generation attending church on a regular basis.

Sincerely,
Whitney Clubine, Lake Orion, Michigan 2008

XXIX. I LEFT THE CHURCH.

Dear Pope Benedict:

The Catholic church has been very important to me and my family. I grew up a Polish Catholic and my First Communion and Confirmation were very joyous events. As a mother of three girls I felt silenced as a woman by some Catholic traditions. I felt I could not be a proper role model to my daughters by following the church's rules and controls. Thus, I decided to join the local Unity Congregational church which I feel honors and respects all cultures and religions. No one is considered better than anyone else. In my opinion the true center of all religious teaching is love and non-judgmental behavior. Jesus taught us to judge no one and love our enemies.

Things are constantly changing but I felt at the time that Catholics considered themselves the chosen religion and were superior to others; they would judge, excommunicate and force spouses to convert their mates to become Catholic.

If women had more positions of authority in the church, it would be more balanced and maybe some of the long-time hidden crimes just being disclosed in the last few years would not have been carried out.

I believe that everyone with different perspectives can work together to change and make the Catholic church healthy and spiritual. To make the change needed it would take the same adjustments corporations make; there is a need for a more diverse hierarchy with a mix of various ideas from men and women in power. Thank you for the work you do.

Sincerely,
Lori VanSloten, 2008, Bloomfield Hills, Michigan

XXX SEMINARIAN SPEAKS OUT.

Dear Pope Benedict:

I would like to apologize beforehand for anything foolish or irreverent I might say. I do not mean any kind of insult or slight to you or the Church by the following remarks. If in any way I offend Your Holiness or anything you stand for, find it in your heart to forgive me.

Firstly, I request your time and patience as I explain my family background. I was born and raised in India, and became an official member of the Syro-Malankara Rite when I was about six years old, although I had attended the Catholic Mass before that time. Despite all the troubles and trials I faced, which included an eight year struggle with asthma, financial difficulties, and ailing parents, I can say with all confidence that it was God who guided me through these problems. He gave me the courage and strength to follow the right path and make the right choices so far in my life, and I pray that He will continue to do so for the rest of my life. He brought my family and me to the United States about seven and a half years ago, which has further aided me in becoming close to Him. In gratitude for His abundant blessings and mercy, I have decided to offer all that I have, including myself, to Christ and His people. I believe I have received the call to become a servant of Christ and I desire to serve Him and His Church through a vocation to the priesthood.

Secondly, I would like to express my sincere thanks and deep respect to you for maintaining Catholic beliefs and principles in front of the whole world. In this changing world, where morals are seen as options and fellow humans as means to personal ends, you continue to shine as the light of Christ from the mountain. It is by this light that people continue to have hope for this world and the people in it. Moreover, I would like to congratulate you for bringing peace and understanding between religions through meetings and synods.

I adhere to the Catholic teachings on abortion, euthanasia, birth control and agree with the Late Pope John Paul II in saying that all three are the fruits of the same tree. I also support the requirement for celibacy for the priesthood for various reasons, but in particular, because I believe the notion of "no celibacy = more priests" is wrong. If the celibacy requirement is dropped, the uniqueness of priesthood is removed in that some are sacrificing everything for the priesthood, while others are free to marry and have children. Moreover, I believe that the number of priests will remain about the same, since in my view, the number of priests and seminarians who want the celibacy requirement and join, will offset the number of incoming seminarians who want to become married priests and leave.

More and more, Catholicism is being seen as an evil institution with a strict, male-dominated hierarchy of conservatives who are out of touch with the changing society. This false view can be attributed to a sweeping wave of ignorance and false information that seems to be going on today. In order to show the true face of the Church, I believe it is important to educate the laity and the public in general about the basic tenets of the Roman Catholic Church and the reasons for the said tenets. Many ridicule Catholic teachings due to its appearance as being old-fashioned and out of touch with today's society. I believe this can be removed through education and information campaigns, thus not only helping the image of the Church, but also teaching the laity about the Church teachings. The information campaign can also show the world the ways in which the Catholic church provides for society, whether it is through charity and education, or service institutions.

The alarming decrease in the number of youth who attend Holy Mass is evident, especially in the developed world. An increased appeal for materialism and the lack of focus on the spiritual matters have brought this about. To them, the Mass is boring and is seen as a chore. They see the liturgy as something that is being done by those who have nothing else to do. The effects seem to be even disconcerting: life appears meaningless, they yearn to experience something that will light a spark and enliven them; they find short termed satisfaction through deviant acts, which include alcohol, drugs, and promiscuous sex. This also can be eradicated through education. The youth should be taught about the meaning of the liturgy, the significance of the structure of the liturgy, and its uniqueness. Moreover, both parents and religious should be advised to encourage the youth to understand the liturgy rather than just recite it. This could also result in an increase in the number of seminarians.

I agree with some of society's views that women are not experiencing a high status in the Church, but I disagree with them on how it can be changed. While the society advocates for women priests and bishops, I advocate for a more Church-doctrine-linked method of making prominent and visible the positions of nuns, religious sisters, and consecrated virgins. I also believe that prayer and scripture reading seem to be declining, even in devout Catholic homes. The places where vocations seem to thrive the most also give the impression of having a better focus on prayer life and scripture reading. An increased focus on both these areas can help the Church and society in many ways, especially by training individuals with a better sense of morality and ethics.

Sincerely,
Jerry Mathew, Oakland University, Rochester, Mi., 2008

XXXI. REPORT ON BAD EXPERIENCE

Dear Pope Benedict:

    I would like to express to you how I feel about the Catholic religion. I am not a Catholic, but was married to a Catholic [man] and was in close contact with his family who were practicing Catholics. I would like to start by expressing how sad I thought it was that our marriage was not recognized by the Catholic church because I was not Catholic. My husband did not practice his faith but I did attend services at the Nazarene church. My mother-in-law was never accepting of me due to my non-Catholic religious tradition. My children were not baptized and it saddens me to hear that some believe that non-baptized children are not going to heaven. My children are wonderful and very active in our church [Nazarene]; they love God and love attending church. I cannot believe for a moment that they are not going to heaven. I also question why as a believer and a person who has a personal relationship with Christ, I was never able to participate in communion with my family at Mass. I spoke with the priest at my in-laws parish and asked why there were no bibles in church. The bible is the living word of God and speaks to all who read it with an open heart and open mind. Why is bible reading not encouraged?

                    Thanks and God Bless,
                    Hilarie Williams, 2008, Royal Oak, Michigan

XXXII. MAJOR CHANGE REQUIRED TO SAVE CHURCH

Dear Pope Benedict,

It appears you have been chosen to guide our church through very difficult times. The stress must be tremendous, but it is also a great opportunity for you to use the power given to you to bring the church and its practices back to the message Jesus preached and told us to follow.

The sex abuse scandals have had enormous coverage, so I will not deal with them in this letter. The first issue that I would like to address is the declining number of church members. From what I have read and heard, one of the ways church leaders propose to deal with this is to "Reform the Reform." After Vatican II many religious and lay people left the church. The answer from "the top" seems to be that if the church goes back to the practices in place when the numbers were high, all will be well again. Bringing back the Latin mass, the priest with his back to the congregation, the communion rail will do just fine. The reasons stated in favor of this are to, "bring back the sense of mystery." I have read that the priests coming out of the seminaries today want to go in this direction. America magazine printed an article showing that the younger priests were complaining that the "older priests have ruined the church" for them.

After WWII, analysts studied the education of students in the U.S. and they found that students with high grades had high self-esteem. Therefore the field of education changed its practices to ensure all students had good self-

esteem. It never occurred to them that the reason these students had high self-esteem is because they worked hard for their grades. The people interpreting this study had it backwards. Today surveys indicate our students have high self-esteem regarding their grades, even though their grades are low.

I bring this up to make the point that the "Reform the Reform movement" also has it backwards. A major point I have yet to see addressed is the difference of the people in the pews before and after Vatican II. The scriptures were closed to many lay people; many faithful did not have advanced degrees and they depended upon the clergy to tell them what to do and believe. I wonder if the laity who left at this time were upset that responsibility was placed upon them. No longer could they "just follow the rules and be guaranteed a place in heaven."

When the scriptures were opened to the laity, many priests and church leaders started bible study lessons for their parishioners. The scriptures have now been an integral part of many church members' lives for over forty years. I have 32-year-old twins with advanced degrees and who have studied Scripture growing up in their catechism classes. Our pastor taught scripture through his homilies. As adults, do they go to church each week? No, but they go at certain times. Do they live their lives according to the teachings of Jesus? Absolutely yes!

My son wanted to leave his job at one of the top accounting firms. When I asked why, his response was, "They are destroying my soul." This is a man you are trying to reach and keep. He is not unusual; there are many like him. They are intelligent, deep, intuitive and possess wisdom due to the times and culture they must face.

The people before the reform did not know what Jesus emphasized during his ministry. We only got bits and pieces, and that through a very biased viewpoint. Do church leaders really believe that people like my children will attend church where the prayers are in a sacralized language (New Roman Missal) and the priest has his back to them? The church will never have a congregation like the parishes before Vatican II. Why is this crucial point being ignored?

This generation has seen more technology change than all previous generations combined. They hear the blatant contradiction of church teaching that states science cannot be used to create life (in vitro), but must be used to prolong life through feeding tubes. It is pure insult to their intelligence, logic and most of all faith in Jesus who showed compassion in his dealing with people.

Why are the numbers down? I suggest it is because the membership has become educated and church leaders cannot keep up with modern problems, e.g., sexual abuse, AIDS. People now know how Jesus wanted His followers to live and they do not see that happening in a church filled with clergy committed to wealth, secrecy, and attention to the externals. They know that these are the very things Jesus criticized in the leadership of his religion based in Jerusalem. They know how Jesus took a whip to clear "my father's house" of those who were making it a "den of thieves." You and the people you have surrounded yourself with have tried to place the blame on the media. Perhaps you should see the media is the whip Jesus is using today.

Paul insisted on making accommodations for the gentiles. He was given a new Gospel. The church structure made accommodations to fit the patriarchal structure of Rome during the 2nd century. But under the direction of Paul, women were heads of house-churches and deacons in the 1st century. Women today are not limited by society. There are no cultural, historical or spiritual reasons for women to be banned from priesthood. Jesus and Paul treated women as equals, so why is that not happening?

If you want the Catholic Church to grow again, the church needs to make accommodations to fit the people of this generation. Paul set the precedent for this practice. Jesus made it clear that the law was made for the people. He accused the leadership in his time for doing the opposite. Jesus used the law to free people, not to bind them. This is the model followed by the Council of Jerusalem, 50 A.D. As the pope, you have the power to do the same. As the pope, it is your duty to do so. Jesus taught that the leaders of the church are to serve. This is what the priests who stayed did after Vatican II. Their paradigm of church and their vocation was turned upside down. They should be thanked for having the courage to take responsibility for preparing people for change, and educating the laity about scripture. These men are the church heroes of today. All of them whom I know or have read, all believe women should be ordained. How could they not? They have studied and know the history of the church. Women deacons were active in the 5th century according to the Church Fathers.

Why did so many of the clergy leave after Vatican II? I doubt it was because they would improve their economic status, although perhaps that is the reason for the departure of some. Perhaps they entered religious life because of their love of God and desire to serve Him. Now they discovered people could serve God in any capacity. If they "wanted the one thing," which was to serve God, they could listen and follow the Spirit to where they were now being called—many to a vocation where their gifts could be used and serve more people in different ways.

There are scripture scholars who state that human temptations could be summarized as follows: Power, Pride and Possessions. The temptation to create bread from stone—possessions. Pride—throw yourself off the cliff because IF you are the Son of God you will not be harmed. Power—take over political power under the guise of doing more to help people temporarily vs. the greater power over sin and death.

The reason I bring this up is because in Time's recent article of June 7, 2010 you stated that your main concerns were the church losing pride, power and possessions. "She will no longer be able to fill many of the buildings created in her period of great splendor." "She will lose many of her privileges in society." "It will make her poor and a church of the little people." How can

I not question if you have read the New Testament when I see these words? The entire image of the church you project is found in the Acts of the Apostles. It was how the church developed after the resurrection of Christ. Can you prayerfully imagine the Jesus of the New Testament walking through the Vatican and not wanting to take out his whip again? I do believe the art and artifacts of the early church should be saved and cherished. But the "pomp and circumstances" surrounding the life style of the Vatican is a long way off from Jesus entering Jerusalem on a donkey. What did he wear? How did he travel? How did he serve? Did he use cups made of gold and gems at the Last Supper? If he took the Pharisees to task for wearing their phylacteries for show, what would he say to the hierarchy as it stands today? What is he saying to you through this crisis of membership and growth?

It has been reported that the reason the church does not want to make any changes is because "it would mean the Holy Spirit was not with the prior leadership!" This is offensive to Christians for two major reasons:

1. It presumes that the Holy Spirit speaks only to the Papal leadership.

2. It is not logical or historical in its premise. Paul and the apostles knew how to make accommodations as the membership and culture changed. The Spirit is NOT static. The Spirit is always moving, speaking and guiding.

Jesus spoke of service, prayer and worship. The generation you need to be reaching is the generation who came up with the "What Would Jesus Do?" (WWJD) bracelets. This continues to be their discernment guide. They are looking at the Church to provide support and community in this life style. Filling empty churches and church coffers is not their priority. It is my belief the church needs to align their priorities with the priorities of Jesus and those who wish to follow Him by living his message.

Sincerely,
Denise Anderson, Grosse Pointe Woods, Michigan.

Clergy to convene, discuss Catholic missal changes

Priests concerned about alterations in midst of other church issues
By Annysa Johnson of the Milwaukee Journal Sentinel
Aug. 5, 2010 |

Catholic clergy and lay leaders from around the region will gather in Milwaukee Thursday for a two-day conference that will be, for some, their first in-depth look at the controversial changes ahead in the Catholic liturgy.

The Vatican is issuing its most significant and extensive revision of the Roman Missal—the prayers and texts used in Catholic worship—since the 1960s in an effort said to better reflect the original Latin texts.

But some see the changes, due to be implemented late next year, as unwieldy and unnecessary. And they fear they could further alienate the faithful at a time when the church is already struggling financially and failing to retain members.

"For some people this will be very unsettling," said Father Ken Smits, a Capuchin priest and liturgical scholar who is troubled by the move away from the vernacular to a more stilted, "sacralizing" language.

"The real concern is among the parish priests, who will have to explain something many of them are not in favor of," said Smits. "They'd much rather spend their time in ministry than have to go through this linguistic exercise."

The Archdiocese of Milwaukee workshop is one of 22 around the country aimed at educating clergy and lay leaders on the revisions.

Dean Daniels, director of the archdiocese's Office for Worship, called critics' concerns valid, but said the revision will bring English-speaking Catholics in line with the global church.

"Anytime there are changes, people go through the process of being angry and sad," he said. "But the church has been changing forever. It's a dynamic, living organism."

The Vatican approved the U.S. version of the Missal revision in March. An international petition drive asking English-speaking bishops to slow the implementation using a pilot program has drawn more than 21,000 signatures, including many from Wisconsin.

The new translation, nine years in the making, is the work of the Vatican's Congregation for Divine Worship and Discipline of the Sacraments and a committee of English-speaking bishops and consultants known as Vox Clara, or "Clear Voice."

That alone is troubling to some who see the revisions as part of a systematic dismantling of provisions of the Second Vatican Council, which, among other things, endorsed the celebration of the Mass in the vernacular of the people and gave national bishops conferences authority over translations.

"The fathers of Vatican II said overwhelmingly that we know how to adapt the prayers to our own needs," said Father David Cooper of St. Matthias Parish in Milwaukee and chairman of the Milwaukee Archdiocese Priest Alliance.

The new translation introduces more formal, rarefied language into the liturgy. But Cooper and others who have studied drafts say it ignores English grammar and syntax and introduces terms—"consubstantial," "oblation," "ignominy," to mention a few—unfamiliar to many American Catholics. And some worry it will sow division in the pews.

"You can call it whatever you like, but it's not English," said Cooper.

"The language of prayer is supposed to be evocative, graceful, uplifting," he said. "This reads like clunk-clunk-clunk-bang-boom."

Some pastors have already begun preparing their parishioners for the changes, which will ultimately require an investment in new missals and hymnals.

"Much of the music that has come up over the last 30 years will no longer be useable," said Father Alan Jurkus of St. Alphonsus Parish in Greendale, who sent out a letter this month notifying members of the coming changes.

Jurkus is encouraging parishioners to accept the revision as an opportunity to grow in their faith. But he harbors his own concerns.

"The bottom line for me is why. Why, with everything else that's going on in the church, do we have to rub salt in the wounds?"

To read more The U.S. Conference of Catholic Bishops has created a Web page devoted to the Roman Missal revisions. It can be found at www.usccb.org/ romanmissal.

XXXIII. LEARN TO RESPECT WOMEN LEADERS

Dear Pope Benedict XVI,

What was the Vatican thinking on July 15, 2010 when it called the ordination of women to the priesthood a "grave crime" and on a par with the sexual abuse of children? Both acts are punishable by excommunication. This is not only un-Christian, but is a policy that I am convinced Our Lord Jesus, St. Paul and members of the earliest Christian communities did not believe or endorse.

Sitting at the feet of the teacher was the position of the student and disciple; we see how the Gospel of Luke 10:38-41, shows Mary sitting at the feet of Jesus while he taught his disciples. Mary, clearly then, was his student and disciple.

Before any male proclaimed the good news of Jesus, the Christ, a woman has preceded him: Mary in her "yes" to the angel gave birth to God's son(Luke 1:38). Her cousin Elizabeth greeted her with joy(Luke 1:43); the woman at the well shared the good news with the people in her village (John 4:29); Mary Magdalene proclaimed the good news of the resurrection to the disciples (John 20:18).

In the authentic letters of St. Paul we find again and again women in leadership roles (Phoebe, Prisca, Mary, Junia, Tryphosa, Euodia and others who were leaders of communities). Paul teaches us about the equality of men and women ("There is no longer Jew or Greek, there is no longer slave or free, there is no longer male and female; for all of you are one in Christ Jesus" Gal 3:27-28). Any policy that did not allow both men and women to fully use their gifts from God would have been foreign to Paul and his understanding of the gospel and baptism.

According to the Didascalia (ca. 3rd century) chapter XVI, women deacons had specific roles and duties in the church. From the Didache of the Twelve Apostles, the Didascalia, and later documents we know that women have been leading prayer services for over two thousand years. Women have been in positions of leadership and authority for equally as long. Women have also had roles of Christian service since the days of Jesus and the apostles.

To marginalize, devalue and demonize any person because of their gender is scandalous in light of the good news of Jesus the Christ, whom you say you believe and follow.

As the Pope you are called to be the leader of the Christian world that reflects the gospel values that Jesus taught. We, as Roman Catholics, are called to be as counter cultural as Jesus was. We should be using scripture and the history of Christianity, especially early Christianity, as tools of enlightenment instead of tools of oppression, both of which show just how effective women were in their roles of leaders of service, leaders of prayer and leaders of communities.

I challenge you to stop being the CEO of the institutional Roman Catholic Church and return to the role of being its Shepherd. I challenge you to raise the role of women in our church by allowing them the honor of ordination to both the deaconate and priesthood as I would extend the honor to both gay and

married men as well. I challenge you to allow women to use the gifts that are uniquely theirs for the betterment of the church. Women have been performing these roles for hundreds of years already so I do not think the Holy
Spirit would be the least bit surprised or upset.

In the peace of Christ,
Kathy Desrochers, Rochester, Michigan

Women priests and sex abuse not equal crimes: Vatican

Fri, Jul 16 2010
By Philip Pullella

VATICAN CITY (Reuters)—The Vatican on Friday denied accusations that it viewed the ordination of women as priests and the sexual abuse of minors by clerics as equally criminal.

On Thursday, the Vatican issued a document making sweeping revisions to its laws on sexual abuse, extending the period in which charges can be filed against priests in church courts and broadening the use of fast-track procedures to defrock them.

But while it dealt mostly with pedophilia, it also codified the "attempted ordination of a woman" to the priesthood as one of the most serious crimes against Church law.

The inclusion of both issues in the same document caused a stir among some groups around the world, particularly those favoring a female priesthood.

"The Vatican's decision to list women's ordination in the same category as pedophiles and rapists is appalling . . . ," Erin Saiz Hanna, executive director of the Women's Ordination Conference said. She called the decision "mediaeval at best".

But Monsignor Charles Scicluna, an official in the Vatican's doctrinal department, said there was no attempt to make women's ordination and pedophilia comparable crimes under canon (Church) law.

"This is not putting everything into one basket," Scicluna, the Vatican's internal prosecutor for handling sexual abuse cases, told Reuters in a telephone interview.

"They are in the same document but this does not put them on the same level or assign them the same gravity," said Scicluna, who helped formulate the revisions.

The document was an attempt to update norms concerning "three sets of canonical crimes that are distinct," and whose jurisdiction is reserved to the Congregation for the Doctrine of the Faith, the Vatican's doctrinal department, he said.

CRIME AGAINST MORALITY

While sexual abuse was a "crime against morality," the attempt to ordain a woman was a "crime against a sacrament," he said, referring to Holy Orders (the priesthood). The revisions also updated crimes against the faith such as heresy.

"This should not be interpreted as considering all these crimes to be equal," he said. "They are crimes of a different nature".

The Catholic Church teaches that it cannot ordain women as priests because Christ chose only men as his apostles. Proponents of a female priesthood reject this, saying he was only acting according to the norms of his times.

Some dissenters saw the placing of the two in one document as an attempt by the Vatican to respond to criticism by those who say the cause of at least some sexual abuse can be found in the Church's insistence on a male, celibate priesthood.

"Sexuality is so denied in our Church," said Christian Weisner, a spokesman for the "We Are Church" liberal Catholic reform movement. "The Roman Catholic Church has to revise its sexual teachings because I think that this is the root of pedophile crime," Weisner told Reuters.

Jon O'Brien, president of the U.S.-based group Catholics for Choice, said the Vatican "feels threatened" by a growing movement in the Church that is in favor of a female priesthood.

O'Brien, whose group favors a female priesthood, said that while he understood the technical distinction of different types of Church crimes, putting the two together was another example of what he called bungled communications.

"If there is an opportunity for authorities in the Vatican to shoot themselves in the foot, they do so in both feet," O'Brien told Reuters. (Editing by Philippa Fletcher)

XXXIV. DO WHAT YOU THINK IS RIGHT.

Dear Pope Benedict:

I am not a religious man; I consider myself ethnically Jewish, but do not practice the customs of my faith. I consider myself an agnostic and have never been able to make the leap to faith. I feel I have a strong sense of ethics and morals, yet I am sure they greatly differ from yours.

You have a strong sense of ethics and morals and I do not feel I have the right to pass judgment on these standards. Ultimately, you must do what you think is right, since you as a religious leader, have no obligation to appease the masses. It is your right to interpret the rules of Catholicism as you see fit. It is also inevitable that there will be consequences for your actions.

In closing, I think it is wrong that some people are angry that you were a member of the Hitler Youth Brigade. You were a child.

Sincerely,
Norm Metzger, Royal Oak, Michigan, 2008

[editor's note: Joseph Ratzinger at age 14 became a member of 'Hitler Youth' and, indeed, membership was required after 1939. At age 16 (1943) he was drafted by the Nazi armed forces and served in the German anti-aircraft corps. Various health issues kept him from involvement in a rigorous military program. However, it is hard to believe that he was not instrumental in the killing of allied forces in World War II. He, like many other German soldiers, deserted the Nazi army in 1945 and was placed in a POW camp until the end of the war. After the war, he was allowed to return home where he continued his education, entered a seminary, and was ordained a priest. Many in the West forgave him for being a Nazi soldier but some argue that his Nazi past should have excluded him from becoming pope.]

CONCLUSION AND COMMENT

These letters show that college students hold a wide variety of opinions about the pope, the Catholic church, and its teachings. The students clearly possess a great deal of knowledge about church affairs even though at times certain positions are stated poorly or incorrectly. They write with passion. Some are pleased with the way things are, e.g., "you are handling everything rather well" (Seibert) but others voice disappointment: the Catholic church needs to "get its head out of the history books, and catch up with society" (Bussard). There are moderating voices in these letters and inspiring stories about the church's accomplishments. Internal problems such as women in leadership roles, married clergy, and questionable teachings are well known to the scholar of religion. In general, these students know what they are talking about. External church blunders such as offensive statements about Islam, rigid homophobic theologies, and lengthy inaction regarding the AIDS-condom conflict show the pope is sliding deeper into the quagmire of church ideology, not faith-inspired religion. Many of these letters call for action and change, and here is a list of their concerns.

- The Church should ordain women to the priesthood
- Allow married priests; celibacy should be optional
- Improve weekend liturgy
- Reach out to alienated youth
- Allow the use of condoms to prevent spread of AIDS
- Reform divorce-remarriage policies
- Respect gay and lesbian Catholics
- Reject legalistic and rule-based Christianity

The $3 billion dollar cost of the priest sex abuse crisis was an eye-opener to many.[4] The pope is beginning to move forward on the issue of global climate change, but inaction on other problems make young people wonder about Benedict's ability to provide answers that would draw Catholics to greater respect for his office and the church he represents.

Ok, so you have read the letters and so now what? It is important to note that a recently published study shows that these sentiments of college students, are found in critiques of Evangelical Christian churches as well. Kinnaman and Lyons[5] found that church outsiders (nonmembers ages 16-29) had some rather negative views about Christians. There are 6 things outsiders do not like about Evangelical Christians:

1. They are hypocritical. They say one thing and do another.
2. They are too focused on getting converts. They stress salvation and being born again to the detriment of Christian service.
3. Anti-homosexual. Christians are bigoted against gays and lesbians and want to cure them, not accept them.
4. Too sheltered. They are simplistic, old fashioned, and boring.
5. Too political. They are overly connected to conservative, right-wing causes.
6. They are judgmental. Christians are too quick to condemn others without knowing more about their opinions.

I find that this study of Evangelicals and their alleged short-comings has many similarities with the letters written to Pope Benedict. Students write about gays and lesbians whom many feel have been mistreated by the Catholic church. Many college students feel unwelcome in church because of their youthful lifestyles and behavior. The Catholic church lacks adequate change mechanisms to resolve its problems and it is too judgmental for the most part, according to students who wrote letters.

---

4   http://www.medindia.net/news/US-Roman-Catholic-Church-or-Pedophile-Club-67308-1.htm; retrieved Oct. 3, 2010

5   David Kinnaman and Gabe Lyons, *Unchristian* (Grand Rapids, Mi: Baker Books), p. 29.

Should the pope just stay the course? Things will get better, right? They can't get much worse. The recent survey findings (n= 35,000) by the Pew Forum on Religion and Public Life offer a different perspective.[6] Not only is the Catholic church looking bad and is probably a dysfunctional organization, it is losing members at an alarming rate. Could these concepts be related? The Catholic Church has lost more adherents than any other religious group studied by the Pew Forum: about one-third (31%) of Americans reported they were raised Catholic, but only 24% indicated they are still members of the Catholic church at the time of the study. The data lead to the following general conclusion by scholars: "One-in-ten American adults is a former Catholic."[7] Can we put a number with this finding? Just how many Catholics have been lost? There are approximately 236 million adults (18 and over) in the U.S. today (2009 census data) and 10 % of that number is 23.6 million. Yes, there are about 23-24 million adults in the USA who used to be Catholic! This is an astounding finding, but for many these numbers are hard to fathom.

In order to portray the dire consequences facing the Catholic church, I have prepared a brief case study analysis of Catholic church life in a moderate-sized diocese in the Midwest. The Milwaukee Archdiocese was once a thriving Catholic metropolis and in the early 1960s boasted that it had one of the highest percentages of Catholic faithful in the U.S. But times have changed in the last 50 years. Its major theological seminary has closed, the number of priests per parishioner has shrunk by 50%. The diocese has been facing serious financial problems for several years and in January 2011 Archbishop Listecki filed for chapter 11 bankruptcy protection. A ten year study using archdiocesan data has revealed the following trends.

---

6   "Americans change Faiths," New York Times, February 25, 2008

7   http://religions.pewforum.org/reports

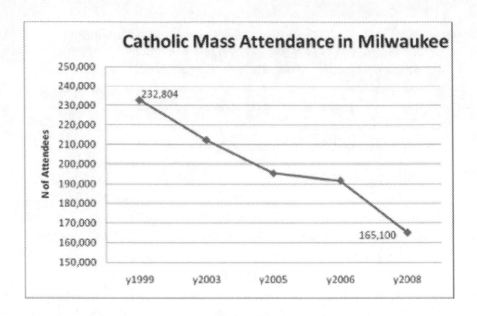

Ten years ago the diocese, on average, could count on about 233,000 people to attend weekend masses. The diocese does its own counts to establish these figures so we are using their institutional data. Ten years later church records show that only about 165,000 Catholics attend weekend services. It is clear that the number of active Catholics is shrinking and so are the number of truly active church-goers who pay the bills. This is really a microcosm of the Pew study findings referenced above. Due to lack of money many schools and churches have had to close in the USA; numerous social services are no longer available. It was not surprising that the Milwaukee Archdiocese declared bankruptcy in January, 2011, and became the 8th Catholic diocese to do so. Without drastic changes, the next ten years will be even more horrendous for the Catholic church and its members.

Finally, the Boston Archdiocese has signaled it is on the verge of collapse when it revealed the following data to the public. About 40 percent of its parishes will not be able to pay all their bills this fiscal year. The number of active priests will plummet from 316 to 178 in the next ten years. Only about "17 percent of local Catholics now attend Mass."[8] Little wonder why Hans Küng stated recently that the church is in crisis.

The message has been laid out for Roman Catholic officials to read and ponder. The narratives of college and university students state what the hard data have been saying all along. This church is struggling and must face reality. It needs to change its ways. Let's hope the words of Suzanne Sataline, written in 2008, are not prophetic, namely, that few Catholics "believe the pontiff, who will turn 81 years old during the trip [to the U.S.], has the time or inclination to try to fix the problems sapping the American church."[9] I am sure the U.S. students who wrote these letters hope someone is listening.

R. John Kinkel
October, 2011

---

8   USA Today, "Boston Archdiocese," USA Today, June 3, 2011.
9   Suzanne Sataline, The Wall Street Journal, April 14, 2008, p. A3.